I0413520

science for a changing world

Prepared in cooperation with the Calaveras County Water District and the California Department of Water Resources

Test Drilling and Data Collection in the Calaveras County Portion of the Eastern San Joaquin Groundwater Subbasin, California, December 2009–June 2011

By Loren F. Metzger, John A. Izbicki, and Joseph M. Nawikas

Open-File Report 2012–1049

U.S. Department of the Interior
U.S. Geological Survey

U.S. Department of the Interior
KEN SALAZAR, Secretary

U.S. Geological Survey
Marcia K. McNutt, Director

U.S. Geological Survey, Reston, Virginia: 2012

For more information on the USGS—the Federal source for science about the Earth, its natural and living resources, natural hazards, and the environment—visit *http://www.usgs.gov* or call 1–888–ASK–USGS

For an overview of USGS information products, including maps, imagery, and publications, visit *http://www.usgs.gov/pubprod*

To order this and other USGS information products, visit *http://store.usgs.gov*

Suggested citation:
Metzger, L.F., Izbicki, J.A., and Nawikas, J.M., 2012, Test drilling and data collection in the Calaveras County portion of the Eastern San Joaquin Groundwater Subbasin, California, December 2009–June 2011: U.S. Geological Survey Open-File Report 2012-1049, 26 p.

Contents

Figures

Tables

Test Drilling and Data Collection in the Calaveras County Portion of the Eastern San Joaquin Groundwater Subbasin, California, December 2009—June 2011

By Loren F. Metzger, John A. Izbicki, and Joseph M. Nawikas

Abstract

Two multiple-well monitoring sites were drilled in the Calaveras County portion of the Eastern San Joaquin Groundwater Subbasin, about 100 miles east of San Francisco, California, during December 2009 and January 2010. Site 3N/9E-12G1-4 was drilled to a depth of 503 feet below land surface (bls), and four wells were installed. Site 4N/9E-36A1-3 was drilled to a depth of 400 feet bls, and three wells were installed. Lithologic and geophysical data collected during test drilling indicated the presence of volcanic sands interspersed with lahar deposits that are characteristic of the Mehrten Formation to about 420 feet bls at site 12G1-4, and the presence of volcanic sands interspersed with clay that are characteristic of the Valley Springs Formation at site 36A1-3. In January 2010, water levels at site 12G1-4 ranged from 120 to 127 feet bls (the shallowest well at the site, 12G4, screened from 90 to 110 feet bls, was dry). Between May and November 2010, water levels declined as much as 22 feet in wells 12G1 and 12G2, the deepest wells at this site, and declined about 6 feet in shallower well 12G3. During this same period, water-levels declined less than 8 feet in the three wells at site 36A1-3. Water levels in all monitoring wells recovered to near-May-2010 levels by mid-spring 2011. Dissolved solids in the six sampled monitoring wells (residue on evaporation) ranged from 154 to 239 milligrams per liter (mg/L); arsenic concentrations ranged from 1.8 to 13 micrograms per liter (µg/L), and were greater than the U.S. Environmental Protection Agency Maximum Contaminant Level (MCL) for arsenic of 10 µg/L in well 36A2. The oxygen-18 ($\delta^{18}O$) and deuterium (δD) stable-isotopic composition of water from the six monitoring wells and from nine domestic and public-supply wells sampled as part of this study ranged from -6.7 to -8.2 per mil ($\delta^{18}O$), and -50 to -60 per mil (δD), and was consistent with values expected for water recharged in the lower altitudes of the Sierra Nevada. Well 36A3, the shallowest well at site 36A1-3, was the only well that contained measurable tritium—indicative of water recharged after 1952. Carbon-14 activities from the six monitoring wells ranged from 76.0 to 18.9 percent modern carbon, and groundwater ages (time since recharge), not corrected for chemical reactions, ranged from 2,200 to 13,400 years before present.

Introduction

The study area is the Camanche/Valley Springs portion of the Eastern San Joaquin Groundwater Subbasin in Calaveras County, about 100 mi east of San Francisco (fig. 1). The population of Calaveras County increased from 20,700 in 1980 to 45,600 in 2010 (California Department of Finance, 2011), with a projected population in Calaveras County of 56,300 in 2020 (California Department of Finance, 2007). Although the area has abundant surface-water supplies, water is supplied to rural residents predominantly by domestic wells, or by public-supply wells operated by small community service-districts. In some areas, especially near Burson (fig. 1), groundwater-level declines resulting from pumping have caused wells to go dry (Ed Pattison, Calaveras County Water District, oral commun., 2010). Although local groundwater generally is suitable for agricultural, domestic, and public-supply uses, some groundwater-quality characteristics might limit future water development. These limiting groundwater-quality characteristics include the presence of naturally occurring high concentrations of dissolved solids, iron, and arsenic, and increasing nitrate concentrations (Ed Pattison, Calaveras County Water District, oral commun., 2010) associated with overlying land uses, including agriculture and on-site wastewater treatment systems (septic systems) associated with residential development. At present, there is only limited groundwater monitoring in this part of the Eastern San Joaquin Groundwater Subbasin, and most data are collected from domestic wells for which geologic or well-construction data are often unavailable. Without groundwater-monitoring data, planning and management by local agencies will be difficult, and groundwater availability and quality may limit future growth in some areas (Water Resources and Information Management Engineering, 2007).

Purpose

The U.S. Geological Survey (USGS), in cooperation with the Calaveras County Water District (CCWD) and the California Department of Water Resources (CDWR), undertook this study to improve understanding of aquifer conditions in the Camanche/Valley Springs study area. The purpose of this report is to describe the results of test drilling, monitoring-well construction, and data collection at two monitoring sites in the Camanche/Valley Springs area of the Eastern San Joaquin Groundwater Subbasin. The report provides some interpretation of these data, supplemented by existing data from wells that have either long-screened intervals, or unknown construction; existing wells were considered inadequate by the cooperators for the purpose of monitoring groundwater conditions in the study area.

Geohydrology

The Camanche/Valley Springs study area comprises 80 mi^2 of land in the foothills of the Sierra Nevada. The area is between 200 and 1,200 ft in altitude. Climate is characterized by cool, wet winters and warm, dry summers, with average daily temperatures of 46 °F in January, and 78°F in June (University of California, 2010). Average annual precipitation is 22 in. at Camp Pardee, located just east of the Camanche Reservoir. Most precipitation falls between November and April. Annual precipitation varies from year-to-year, ranging from less than 10 to almost 50 in. for the 60-year period of record at Camp Pardee (fig. 2). The eastern and northeastern boundaries of the study area are defined by the boundary of alluvial valley-fill deposits of the Eastern San Joaquin Groundwater Subbasin with resistant hard rocks of the Sierra Nevada. The northwestern boundary of the study area is defined by the Calaveras-Amador County line. The western and southern boundaries of the study area are defined by the Calaveras-San Joaquin County line.

Several major rivers pass through or near the study area. The Mokelumne River located just north of the study area (fig. 1) drains the higher altitudes (greater than 5,000 ft) of the Sierra Nevada. Flow on the Mokelumne River is regulated by management of Camanche Reservoir and Lake Pardee (Water Resources and Information Management Engineering, 2007). Water from these reservoirs is delivered by the East Bay Municipal Water District to several cities in the eastern part of the San Francisco Bay area. The Calaveras River drains lower altitudes (less than 5,000 ft) of the Sierra Nevada than the Mokelumne River and bisects the southern end of the study area. Flow on the Calaveras River is regulated upstream of the study area by the New Hogan Reservoir, operated by the U.S. Army Corps of Engineers (Water Resources and Information Management Engineering, 2007) (fig. 1). Water from New Hogan Reservoir is used primarily by urban and agricultural interests downstream of the study area in San Joaquin County, except for about 3,500 acre-ft/yr used by CCWD (Water Resources and Information Management Engineering, 2007). There are no other perennial streams in the study area, but there are a number of intermittent streams, such as Bear Creek (fig. 1). Some of these streams have been dammed to form small reservoirs, such as Wallace Lake (fig. 1). These small reservoirs are used for water supply and recreational purposes. The water supply from some of the area's reservoirs is supplemented by groundwater pumping or by surface water imported from outside the study area (Jason Preece, California Department of Water Resources, written commun., 2011).

The area is underlain by volcanic deposits consisting of andesitic sands interbedded with lahar and fluvial deposits of the Mehrten Formation (Curtis, 1954) (fig. 3). Lahar deposits within the Mehrten Formation are resistant to erosion and form flat-lying ridgetops characteristic of this part of the Sierra Nevada foothills. The Mehrten Formation thins to the east and is underlain by the Valley Springs Formation, which is exposed at land surface in the eastern part of the study area. The Valley Springs Formation includes volcanic deposits consisting of rhyolitic sands and clays (Curtis, 1954). Both the Mehrten and Valley Springs Formations are permeable and yield water to wells—especially in places where fluvial units are present in the Mehrten Formation. The Valley Springs Formation overlies the less permeable sandstone and claystones of the Ione Formation, which forms the effective base of fresh water (Creely and Force, 2007). Groundwater in the Ione Formation is predominantly saline, having dissolved-solids concentrations as high as 1,070 mg/L (Water Resources and Information Management Engineering, 2003).

Groundwater recharge to the Mehrten and Valley Springs Formations occurs in the study area primarily as infiltration of precipitation and seasonal streamflow. Groundwater movement is from the east to west. A bedrock high in the northern part of the study area separates Camanche Reservoir from permeable deposits underlying most of the study area. Water levels in adjacent parts of the Eastern San Joaquin Groundwater Subbasin (west of the study area) are declining because pumping exceeds recharge (CDM, Inc., 2001). Figure 4 shows data for seven wells (California Department of Water Resources, 2011) with records dating back to the late 1940s; average annual declines in these wells range from 0.6 to 1.2 ft/yr (California Department of Water Resources, 2011).

Test Drilling, Geophysical Logs, and Monitoring-Well Installation

Two multiple-well monitoring sites were constructed during December 2009 and January 2010. The sites are approximately 4.5 mi (3N/9E-12G1-4) and 2.5 mi (4N/9E-36A1-3) southwest of Burson, Calif., respectively (fig. 1). Site 12G1-4 is located on property that includes a golf course irrigated with local groundwater. Site 36A1-3 is located on property partially used for vineyards irrigated with both groundwater and surface water diverted from Bear Creek. The boreholes were drilled using the mud-rotary method by a U.S. Geological Survey drill rig and crew to depths of 503 ft (3N/9E-12G1-4) and 400 ft (4N/9E-36A1-3) below land surface (bls). After the boreholes for site 3N/9E-12G1-4 and 4N/9E-36A1-3 were drilled, geophysical logs were collected. Lithologic data and geophysical logs were used to select depth intervals for well installation. Changes in the magnitude and general characteristics of geophysical logs, interpreted with lithologic data collected during drilling, were used to identify changes in subsurface geology (see section. "Geophysical Logs").

Four monitoring wells were installed at site 3N/9E-12G1-4, and three monitoring wells were installed at site 4N/9E-36A1-3 (figs. 5A and 5B) (table 1). The monitoring wells were constructed by using threaded 2-inch diameter, schedule 40, PVC casing installed at different depths in the same borehole (figs. 5A–B). Each of the monitoring wells has a screen perforated interval of 10–20 ft in length. The annular space around the well screens were packed in graded sand and were separated vertically by low-permeability bentonite grout pumped through the tremie pipe into the borehole. A 20-ft-thick concrete surface seal was pumped into the upper 20 ft of the borehole to comply with County regulations (Municipal Code Corporation, 2008). Wells were developed by using an air-compressor shortly after installation to remove drilling mud. Multiple-well sites constructed in this manner provide depth-specific water-level and water-quality data in complex aquifer systems.

Geophysical Logs

Geophysical logs, including caliper, natural gamma ray, electrical resistivity, spontaneous potential, and sonic porosity, were collected after the borehole was drilled, but before well construction.

Caliper Logs – The caliper logs (figs. 5A-B) show the diameter of the borehole. The borehole diameter can occasionally be greater than the diameter of the drill bit (8 or 10-inch) where gravels or other loose material has fallen into the borehole (Schlumberger, 1972). Lahar deposits within the aquifer deposits also might fracture and fall into the borehole during drilling, increasing the borehole diameter.

Natural Gamma Ray – Natural gamma logs (figs. 5A-B) measure the decay of naturally occurring radionuclides, primarily potassium-40 (but also uranium and thorium), within aquifer materials. Gamma logs, in conjunction with lithologic data, may identify the presence of potassium-rich clays or other minerals, such as potassium feldspar, within aquifer deposits. Changes in the magnitude or general characteristics of the natural gamma log also can be used to identify changes in geologic units and formation contacts.

Electrical Logs – Electrical-resistivity logs (figs. 5A–B), such as the 64-inch (long normal) and 16-inch (short normal) logs, measure the resistance of geologic materials and interstitial fluids to an induced electric current (Schlumberger, 1972). The number refers to the electrode spacing within the logging tool used to induce and receive the current. The greater the electrode spacing, the farther the electrical current will penetrate into the surrounding material. More-resistive values are commonly associated with coarser grained deposits, or water having low dissolved-solids concentrations. Unsaturated and consolidated materials are usually more resistive than saturated sand, silt, or clay. Changes in the difference between the resistivity measured by the 64-inch and 16-inch resistivity curves relate to how far conductive drilling mud penetrated into the material surrounding the borehole, and are an indicator of the permeability of the deposits. The spontaneous-potential log (also referred to as the self-potential or SP log) measures the electrical potential between geologic deposits and a grounded voltage at the surface. Fine-grained deposits with high dissolved-solids concentrations will generate one charge, and coarse-grained deposits with low dissolved-solids concentrations will generate a different charge (Schlumberger, 1972). When differences in lithology are accounted for, changes in the spontaneous-potential log can be used to identify changes in water quality within aquifer units.

Sonic Porosity Logs – Sonic porosity data (figs. 5A–B) are generated from sonic logs that measure the speed of sound waves within geologic materials surrounding the borehole. Sound waves travel faster through consolidated deposits than through less consolidated deposits, and these differences can be used to infer changes in geologic material characteristics. Porosity values inferred from sonic logs, using an empirical equation developed by Wyllie and others (1956), are used for comparisons in the borehole and might not reflect actual aquifer porosity values.

Log Interpretation

The lithologic and geophysical data collected from the two boreholes were different. The deeper, southern borehole (12G1-4) (fig. 5A) contained more gravel than the northern borehole (36A1-3), and numerous thin, resistive (less permeable) layers possibly representing lahar units. Deposits at this southern site, composed of volcanic sand, fluvially sorted gravels, and lahar deposits characteristic of the Mehrten Formation, appear to be present to a depth of about 420 ft bls. In comparison, the deep parts of site 12G1-4 and the shallow parts of site 36A1-3 contained more volcanic sand interspersed with more clay, and there were fewer resistive layers indicative of fluvial gravel deposits (fig. 5B); this data is characteristic of the Valley Springs Formation. The presence and identity of other formations at site 36A1-3 is uncertain, but changes in lithology and geophysical properties corresponding to depths of about 150 and 310 ft bls (fig. 5B) may represent the top and bottom, respectively, of the Valley Springs Formation.

Lithologic data and geophysical logs collected as part of this study are on file at the U.S. Geological Survey office in San Diego, California.

Groundwater-Level Data

Wells at each site were equipped with pressure transducers, and water levels were measured from January 2010 to June 2011. The pressure transducers were serviced quarterly. During servicing, data were retrieved and manual water-level measurements were made to ensure that the pressure transducers were functioning properly. Manual water-level measurements were made using a calibrated electric tape.

Groundwater levels at multiple-well site 3N/9E-12G1-4 ranged from about 120 to 127 ft bls in January 2010 and increased with well depth, indicating a downward hydraulic gradient (fig. 6A). The shallowest well at the site (12G4) was dry. Beginning in May 2010, water levels in wells 12G1–3 declined (fig. 6A). Water levels in the two deepest wells (12G1-2) at the site declined by about 22 ft by late October. Water-level declines were less, about 6 ft, in the shallowest well (12G3). Site 12G1-4 is located near several water-supply wells that are screened at depths similar to wells 12G1–2. Water levels in wells 12G1-3 returned to their approximate May 2010 values by mid-spring 2011.

Groundwater levels at multiple-well site 4N/9E-36A1-3 ranged from about 123 to 133 ft bls in wells 36A1–2 at the beginning of transducer measurements in those wells in February 2010 (fig. 6B). The groundwater level in well 36A3 was about 68 ft bls at the beginning of pressure transducer measurements in July 2010 (fig. 6B). For the entire period of record, the lowest water levels were in the intermediate-depth well 36A2, and the highest water levels were in the shallowest well 36A3. This indicates a downward vertical gradient from the shallowest to the intermediate-depth intervals, and an upward vertical gradient from the deepest to the intermediate-depth intervals. Groundwater-level declines at multiple-well site 36A1–3 generally were less than declines measured at site 3N/9E-12G1-4 (fig. 6B). The water level in the deepest well (36A1) declined by almost 8 ft during the 2010 pumping season, but recovered by mid-spring 2011.

Water-Quality Data

One water sample was collected from each monitoring well, except 12G4, at multiple-well sites 3N/9E-12G1-4 and 4N/9E-36A1-3 by the USGS during June or July 2010. Samples were collected for field parameters (temperature, specific conductance, pH, and dissolved oxygen), major ions, trace elements, nutrients, stable isotopes of oxygen and hydrogen, and age-dating constituents including tritium, and carbon-14. Additional samples for the analysis of oxygen and hydrogen isotopes were collected from two surface-water sites by the USGS in March 2011, and from nine domestic and production wells (table 3, fig. 1) by Aperio Inc. in June 2011 (David Wood, Aperio Inc., oral commun., 2011).

Methods of Water Sampling

Monitoring wells at multiple-well sites were purged with a positive displacement pump until three casing volumes were removed and field parameters stabilized. Samples were collected following procedures outlined by the U.S. Geological Survey (2010). Major ions, trace elements, and nutrients were analyzed by the USGS National Water Quality Laboratory (NWQL) in Denver, Colo., following standard methods outlined by Fishman and Friedman (1989), Faires (1993), Fishman (1993), and Jones and Garbarino (1999). Stable isotopes of oxygen and hydrogen were analyzed by the USGS Isotope Laboratory in Reston, Virginia, using methods described by Epstein and Mayeda (1953) and Coplen and others (1991). Tritium was analyzed at the University of Miami by gas scintillation (Thatcher and others, 1977). Carbon-14 was analyzed by the Woods Hole Laboratory in Woods Hole, Mass., using methods described by Beukins (1992).

Samples collected from water-supply wells for this study for the analysis of stable isotopes of oxygen and hydrogen were collected from faucets at or near the well head, and prior to well pressure tanks, when possible. Prior to the collection of these samples, wells were purged until sequential readings of specific conductance, pH, and temperature had stabilized (David Wood, Aperio Inc., oral commun., 2011). Samples collected from surface-water sites were collected directly by immersing the bottle until filled.

General Chemical Characteristics

Dissolved-solids (residue on evaporation) concentrations of water from monitoring wells at the multiple-well sites ranged from 154 to 239 mg/L. The pH ranged from 6.5 to 7.8, although water from most monitoring wells had either slightly acidic or near-neutral pH. Water from monitoring wells was suboxic to oxic, with dissolved-oxygen concentrations between 0.3 and 8.9 mg/L (table 2).

Major-Ion Composition

The major-ion compositions of six water samples from the two multiple-well sites were evaluated using a trilinear diagram (fig. 7). Results from 19 domestic and public-supply wells (completed at depths from 100 to 620 ft bls) collected for the Calaveras County Water District (CCWD) between 2003 and 2006 (Water Resources and Information Management Engineering, 2003, 2007) were included in the trilinear diagram. A trilinear diagram shows the proportions of major cations (calcium, magnesium, and sodium plus potassium) and major anions (carbonate plus bicarbonate, sulfate, and chloride) on a charge-equivalent basis. Cations are plotted on the lower left triangle and anions are plotted on the lower right. The central diamond integrates the data and serves as the basis for comparing water samples having different major-ion compositions. Data from wells in the downgradient (San Joaquin County) part of the Eastern San Joaquin Groundwater Subbasin (Izbicki and others, 2006) were plotted in the background of figure 7 (the locations of these wells are not shown in figure 1). The three water-chemistry groups identified by Izbicki and others (2006) in the downgradient part of the subbasin also are shown in figure 7.

Group 1 includes nine samples from eight wells and is a *calcium-magnesium-bicarbonate* type water. This was the most abundant group identified by Izbicki and others (2006) in the downgradient part of the Eastern San Joaquin Groundwater Subbasin. Six of the wells in this group are located in the northwestern part of the study area (fig. 1). Given the similarity in chemistry, this may be where at least some recharge to alluvial deposits in the downgradient part of the subbasin occurs. Alternatively, the similarity in major-ion chemistry of water to wells in these separate areas may be the result of similar recharge sources, or similar rock/water interaction processes. The origin of the water in this area is discussed in section, "Stable Isotopes of Oxygen and Hydrogen."

Group 2 includes samples from wells 3N/9E-12G1 and 12G2, and is a *sodium-bicarbonate* type water. The composition of these samples is different from most other data in the study area—with higher proportions of sodium plus potassium relative to calcium and magnesium. These data represent major-ion chemistry at deeper depths within the study area. Group 2 is similar to the chemistry of deeper groundwater, some of which is within the Mehrten Formation, in the downgradient part of the Eastern San Joaquin Groundwater Subbasin to the west.

Group 3 includes samples from 15 wells, including all 3 wells at multiple-well site 4N/9E-36A1-3, and well 12G3 at site 3N/9E-12G1-4. This group is a *mixed cation-mixed anion* type water, with sodium as the most abundant cation and chloride as the most abundant anion in water from most wells. Chloride concentrations in some Group 3 wells in the study area are as high as 180 mg/L (Water Resources and Information Management Engineering, 2003). Group 3 is the most common water-quality type in the study area. In the downgradient part of the Eastern San Joaquin Groundwater Subbasin, Group 3 represented high-chloride water originating from the San Joaquin Delta, water from deep deposits underlying the subbasin, and irrigation-return water (Izbicki and others, 2006).

Most Group 3 wells are located in the eastern part of the study area where the water-bearing deposits are thinner. Some deep wells in this area could be affected by upward flow of groundwater with high salinity and chloride concentrations from the underlying Ione Formation. Shallow well 36A3, completed at the water table at site 36A1-3, had the highest chloride concentration of the sampled wells at both multiple-well sites, which may be consistent with recharge of irrigation-return flow from vineyards (Izbicki and others, 2006).

Trace-Element and Nutrient Chemistry

Arsenic concentrations in water from wells in the study area have been reported as high as 120 µg/L (Water Resources and Information Management Engineering, 2003), which is higher than the U.S. Environmental Protection Agency's (USEPA) Maximum Contaminant Level (MCL) for arsenic of 10 µg/L (U.S. Environmental Protection Agency, 2009). Iron and manganese concentrations have been as high as 15,500 and 850 µg/L, respectively (Water Resources and Information Management Engineering, 2003). These concentrations were higher than the USEPA's Secondary MCL for iron and manganese of 300 and 50 µg/L, respectively (U.S. Environmental Protection Agency, 2009). Water-chemistry data from the two multiple-well sites were evaluated to help understand how these constituents vary with depth in the aquifer system underlying the study area.

Arsenic concentrations at the multiple-well sites ranged from 1.8 to 12.8 µg/L, with one well, 36A2, exceeding the MCL for arsenic (table 2). Iron concentrations ranged from less than the reporting limit of 4 to 1,270 µg/L, with one well, 36A3, exceeding the Secondary MCL for iron. Manganese concentrations ranged from 2.2 to 154 µg/L, with two wells, 36A1 and 36A3, exceeding the Secondary MCL for manganese.

Arsenic concentrations were higher at site 4N/9E-36A1-3 than at site 3N/9E-12G1-4. Although arsenic concentrations were higher in deeper wells than in shallower wells (table 2), there was not a consistent increase in arsenic concentrations at both sites with increasing depth. However, reduction/oxidation (redox) and pH conditions may influence arsenic concentrations at these sites. Arsenic concentrations increase with decreasing dissolved-oxygen concentrations and with increasing pH (fig. 8). Given the small, near-neutral range in pH from 6.5 to 7.2 at wells 36A1-3 and 12G2-3, and the lack of alkaline pH greater than 8 that can promote arsenic desorption from the surface of mineral grains, redox conditions may be the primary control acting on arsenic concentrations at these sites. Particularly at wells 36A1-2, decreased redox potential (low concentrations of dissolved oxygen, and high concentrations of iron or manganese, such as occur in well 36A1, consistent with reducing conditions) may indicate dissolution of iron and manganese hydroxides from the surfaces of mineral grains. As these materials dissolve and enter solution, arsenic and other trace elements attached to hydroxide-exchange sites also can enter solution (Izbicki and others, 2008). However, the relatively high arsenic concentration of 9.6 ug/L at well 12G1 may be influenced by comparatively high pH rather than reducing conditions, because this well has pH of 7.8, and has oxic groundwater (high dissolved–oxygen concentrations, low manganese and iron concentrations) rather than reducing conditions.

Nitrate concentrations at the multiple-well sites ranged from less than the reporting level of 0.04 to 2.09 mg/L as nitrogen (table 2). This is similar to results of previous work (Water Resources and Information Management Engineering, 2003) that showed that nitrate concentrations in water from domestic and public-supply wells in the study area do not exceed 1.2 mg/L as nitrogen. Neither multiple-well site was located near residential developments with large concentrations of septic systems; however, the data indicate that high-nitrate concentrations related to septic discharge, although potentially locally important, are not a regional problem in the aquifer in the study area.

Stable Isotopes of Oxygen and Hydrogen

Oxygen-18 (^{18}O) and deuterium (^{2}H or D) are naturally occurring stable isotopes of oxygen and hydrogen. The abundance of heavier oxygen-18 and deuterium relative to isotopically lighter oxygen-16 (^{16}O) and hydrogen (^{1}H) can be used to infer the source and hydrologic history of water. Oxygen-18 and deuterium are expressed in delta notation (δ) as per mil [parts per thousand (‰)] differences in the ratios of $^{18}O/^{16}O$ and $^{2}H/^{1}H$ in samples relative to a standard known as Vienna Standard Mean Ocean Water (VSMOW) (Gat and Gonfiantini, 1981). By convention, the value of VSMOW is 0 per mil. Because the source of much of the world's precipitation is derived from the evaporation of seawater, the $\delta^{18}O$ and δD composition of precipitation throughout the world plots along a line known as the global meteoric water line (GMWL) (Craig, 1961). The $\delta^{18}O$ and δD composition of water along the GMWL results, in part, from differences in the temperature at which water evaporated from liquid to vapor, and at which vapor condensed into precipitation. Differences in the temperature of condensation can occur as a result of condensation at different latitudes, climatic conditions, and altitudes. Water that condensed at cooler temperatures (associated with higher latitudes, cooler climatic regimes, or higher altitudes) is lighter (more negative) than water that condensed at warmer temperatures (associated with lower latitudes, warmer climatic regimes, or lower altitudes). In many areas, the ratios of the stable isotopes of oxygen and hydrogen in groundwater samples plot along a line that is parallel to the GMWL referred to as the local groundwater line (LGWL). Water that has been partly evaporated is enriched in the heavier isotopes, relative to its original composition; these values plot to the right of the LGWL along a line known as the evaporative trend line (Gat and Gonfiantini, 1981).

The $\delta^{18}O$ and δD composition of water from the two multiple-well sites and nine selected wells in the study area ranged from about -6.7 to -8.2 per mil ($\delta^{18}O$) and -50 to -60 per mil (δD) with a median composition of -7.1 and -52 per mil, respectively (fig. 9, table 3). These samples are heavier (less negative) than samples from higher altitudes in the Sierra Nevada (Ingraham, 1991), and reflect the generally lower altitude of precipitation and subsequent groundwater recharge in the study area along the foothills of the Sierra Nevada, compared to precipitation and runoff from higher altitudes. Surface-water samples collected from Bear Creek (BC in fig. 1) and Wallace Lake (WL in fig. 1) also plot below the GMWL, similar to groundwater samples, but are heavier (less negative) than groundwater samples. The sample from Wallace Lake plots to the right of surface water in Bear Creek, possibly due to evaporation (fig. 9).

The isotopic composition of water from wells at the two multiple-well sites becomes lighter with increasing depth (fig. 9), and deeper samples may reflect recharge under cooler and wetter climatic conditions. Because the study area is surrounded by geologic units containing saline groundwater, it is unlikely that these deeper samples could reflect groundwater recharged at higher altitudes that moved along deep flowpaths into the study area. Samples from multiple-well site 4N/9E-36A1-3 include both the isotopically heaviest and isotopically lightest composition of any well sampled in the study area (table 1). In contrast, the isotopic composition of water from other sampled wells in the study area plot within a relatively narrow range of values (fig. 9). $\delta^{18}O$ and δD values from the multiple-well sites represent the range of isotopic composition of groundwater in the study area better than samples from domestic or supply wells with longer perforated intervals.

The isotopic composition of samples from area wells is consistent with groundwater recharge from either direct infiltration of precipitation or infiltration of runoff from local streams. Alternatively, if a significant component of groundwater recharge originated as runoff from the Sierra Nevada captured in Camanche Reservoir, it would have a lighter isotopic composition. The major-ion composition of water from wells in the northwestern part of the study area near Camanche Reservoir (Group 1 in figure 7) probably is the result of local geologic conditions, rather than differences in the source of recharge of the water.

Tritium and Carbon-14

Tritium (^3H) and carbon-14 (^{14}C) were analyzed in samples from the multiple-well sites to estimate the age (time since recharge) of the groundwater.

Tritium is both a naturally occurring and anthropogenic, short-lived (half-life of 12.32 years) (Lucas and Unterweger, 2000), radioactive isotope of hydrogen that can be used to identify relatively young (post-1952) groundwater. Much of the tritium detected in groundwater can be attributed to the atmospheric testing of thermonuclear weapons from 1952 to 1962. Because tritium is part of the water molecule and its concentration is not affected significantly by reactions other than radioactive decay, it is an excellent tracer of recently recharged groundwater (Michel, 1976). For the purposes of this report, groundwater that had a tritium activity greater than the detection level of 0.3 picocuries per liter (pCi/L) was interpreted as having been, in part or in whole, recharged after 1952.

Tritium in water from five of six sampled wells at the two multiple-well sites was less than the 0.3 pCi/L detection level. Water from only the shallowest well, 4N/9E-36A3, had measurable tritium, with a concentration of 0.5 pCi/L (table 1), indicative of water recharged, at least in part, since 1952. The absence of tritium in sampled wells indicates that groundwater recharge in the study area is small, or requires a long time to infiltrate through the unsaturated zone to the water table.

Carbon-14 is a naturally occurring long-lived (half-life of 5,730 years), radioactive isotope of carbon that can be used to identify groundwater ages up to 30,000 years old. Carbon-14 is created in the upper atmosphere by the bombardment of nitrogen atoms by cosmic radiation. Once isolated from the atmosphere, the carbon-14 content in the dissolved carbon steadily decreases through radioactive decay. Carbon-14 data are expressed as percent modern carbon (pmc); 100 pmc is equal to 13.56 disintegrations per minute per gram of carbon (Kalin, 2000). Unlike tritium, carbon-14 is not part of the water molecule, and carbon-14 activities in groundwater can be affected by chemical reactions that generally act to reduce the carbon-14 activity, thereby increasing the apparent age of groundwater.

Measured carbon-14 activities for samples from six monitoring wells (4N/9E-12G1-3 and 3N/9E-36A1-3) ranged from 76.0 to 18.9 pmc (table 2). These carbon-14 activities correspond to apparent ages (uncorrected for chemical reactions) (Kalin, 2000) ranging from about 2,200 to 13,400 years before present. Based on apparent carbon-14 ages, water in the study area becomes progressively older with depth. This corresponds with increasingly negative $\delta^{18}O$ and δD values at each site, indicating that the lighter $\delta^{18}O$ and δD isotopic composition of samples from deeper wells may have originated from precipitation that fell during a wetter and colder climatic period. Groundwater ages are younger at site 4N/9E-12G1-4 than at site 3N/9E-36A1-3 for equivalent depths below land surface, or below the water table throughout the vertical profile through the aquifer; these results indicate that groundwater moves faster vertically at site 4N/9E-12G1-4 than at site 3N/9E-36A1-3. The comparatively old apparent groundwater ages at both sites indicate that either extensive chemical reactions alter carbon-14 activities, groundwater recharge is small (a possibility that would be consistent with the general absence of tritium), or groundwater requires a long time to infiltrate through the unsaturated zone to the water table.

Summary

Two multiple-well sites were installed in the western part of Calaveras County overlying the upgradient area of the Eastern San Joaquin Groundwater Subbasin. Sites 3N/9E-12G1-4 and 4N/9E-36A1-3 were drilled to depths of 503 and 400 ft bls, respectively, and were completed with four and three monitoring wells of varying depths at each site, respectively. Lithologic and geophysical data showed differences in geology between the two well sites. Drilling at site 3N/9E-12G1-4 encountered volcanic sands interspersed with fluvial gravels and lahar deposits characteristic of the Mehrten Formation to a depth of 420 feet. At deeper depths at sites 3N/9E-12G1-4 and 4N/9E-36A1-3, greater occurrence of volcanic sands and clay without gravel layers were characteristic of the Valley Springs Formation.

Water-level monitoring showed water-level declines during the 2010 pumping season of between 6 and 22 ft at multiple-well site 3N/9E-12G1-4, and less than 8 ft at site 4N/9E-36A1-3. Water-level data showed a downward vertical gradient from the shallowest to the intermediate depths at both sites. The downward gradient continued vertically throughout at site 3N/9E-12G1-4 to the deepest depth. In contrast, the vertical gradient at site 4N/9E-36A1-3 was upward from the deepest to the intermediate depth. Although long-term water-level data to the west of the study area show declining water levels over time, the limited duration of water-level monitoring at the two multiple-well sites was insufficient to determine long-term trends.

Water quality in the study area changes with depth and location. Water from wells in the northwestern part of the study area differed chemically from water elsewhere in the study area and was similar to water from much of the Eastern San Joaquin Groundwater Subbasin farther downgradient. Data from the multiple-well sites show that the major-ion composition of water from all three wells at multiple-well site 4N/9E-36A1-3 was a mixed cation-mixed anion type water, but became more bicarbonate rich with depth. The major-ion composition of water from multiple-well site 3N/9E-12G1-4 evolved from a mixed cation-mixed anion type water in the shallowest sampled well (12G3) to a sodium-bicarbonate type water in the two deepest wells (12G1-2). In comparison, samples from water supply wells in the study area were either a calcium-magnesium-bicarbonate or a mixed cation-mixed anion composition. Arsenic concentrations were higher at site 4N/9E-36A1-3 than at site 3N/9E-12G1-4, and arsenic concentrations were higher in deeper wells than in shallow wells. However, there was not a consistent increase in arsenic concentrations at both sites with increasing depth because of differences in redox potential. Redox potential appeared to be the primary control on increasing arsenic concentrations corresponding with decreasing dissolved oxygen and with increasing pH, particularly at wells 36A1-3 and 12G2-3. Alkaline pH and a relatively high arsenic concentration indicate that pH was the primary control at well 12G1.

The $\delta^{18}O$ and δD isotopic composition of water from selected wells reflects groundwater recharge from relatively low-altitude sources along the foothills of the Sierra Nevada, such as direct infiltration of precipitation, or infiltration from intermittent streams that flow through the study area. Isotopically lighter $\delta^{18}O$ and δD values consistent with the expected isotopic composition of water from Camanche Reservoir (Izbicki and others, 2008) were not present in water from wells in the study area. Samples from multiple-well sites shift towards lighter $\delta^{18}O$ and δD values with increasing depth. Isotopically-lighter water might have resulted from recharge that occurred when the climate was cooler and wetter. This conclusion is supported by tritium and carbon-14 data showing an increase in apparent groundwater age with depth. Tritium was detected at activities near the reporting level in water from only one well, 4N/9E-36A3. Apparent groundwater ages (time since recharge) based on carbon-14 activity ranged from about 2,200 to 13,400 years before present. The comparatively old apparent groundwater ages indicate that either extensive chemical reactions alter carbon-14 activities, groundwater recharge is small (a possibility that would be consistent with the general absence of tritium), or recharge requires a long time to infiltrate through the unsaturated zone to the water table.

Acknowledgments

This study was funded by the Calaveras County Water District and the California Department of Water Resources, in cooperation with the U.S. Geological Survey. The authors thank Ed Pattison and the staff of the Calaveras County Water District, the Wallace Community Services District, Wallace Citizens Serving Residents, and David Wood of Aperio Inc. Special thanks to area property owners for permission to install and sample wells.

References Cited

Beukins, R.P., 1992, Radiometric accelerator mass spectrometry—Background, precision, and accuracy, *in* Taylor, R.E., Long, A., and Kra, R.S., eds., 1992, Radiocarbon after four decades: New York, Springer-Verlag, p. 230–239.

California Department of Finance, 2007, Population projections for California and its Counties 2000–2050, by age, gender and race/ethnicity: California Department of Finance, accessed September 26, 2011, at *http://www.dof.ca.gov/research/demographic/reports/projections/p-3/*.

California Department of Finance, 2011, Historical census populations of counties and incorporated cites in California: California Department of Finance, accessed September 26, 2011 *http://www.dof.ca.gov/research/demographic/state_census_data_center/historical_census_1850-2010/view.php*.

California Department of Water Resources, 2011, Water Data Library: California Department of Water Resources, accessed May 20, 2011 *http://www.water.ca.gov/waterdatalibrary/groundwater/index.cfm*.

CDM, Inc., 2001, San Joaquin County Management Plan: Phase 1—Planning analysis and strategy: Sacramento, Calif., Camp, Dresser, and McKee, Inc., variously paged.

Coplen, T.B., Wildman, J.D., and Chem, J.,1991, Improvements in the gaseous hydrogen-water equilibration technique for hydrogen isotope ratio analysis: Analytical Chemistry, v. 63, p. 910–912.

Craig, H., 1961, Isotopic variations in meteoric waters: Science, v. 133, p. 1,702–1,703.

Creely, S., and Force, E.R., 2007, Type region of the Ione Formation (Eocene), Central California—Stratigraphy, paleogeography, and relation to auriferous gravels: U.S. Geological Survey Open-File Report 2006-1378, 65 p.. (Also available at *http://pubs.usgs.gov/of/2006/1378/.*)

Curtis, G.H., 1954, Mode of origin of pyroclastic debris in the Mehrten formation of the Sierra Nevada: California University Publications in Geological Science, v. 29, no. 9, p. 453–502.

Epstein, S., and Mayeda, T., 1953, Variation of O^{18} content of waters from natural sources: Geochimica et Cosmochimica Acta, v. 4, p. 213–224

Faires, L.M., 1993, Methods of analysis by the U.S. Geological Survey National Water Quality Laboratory—Determination of metals in water by inductively coupled plasma-mass spectrometry: U.S. Geological Survey Open-File Report 92-634, 28 p.

Fishman, M.J., and Friedman, L.C., eds., 1989, Methods for determination of inorganic substances in water and fluvial sediments: U.S. Geological Survey Techniques of Water-Resources Investigations, book 5, chap. A1, 545 p.

Fishman, M.J., 1993, Methods of analysis by the U.S. Geological Survey National Water Quality Laboratory—Determination of inorganic and organic constituents in water and fluvial sediments: U.S. Geological Survey Open-File Report 93-125, 217 p. *http://pubs.er.usgs.gov/usgspubs/ofr/ofr93125.*

Gat, J.R., and Gonfiantini, R., 1981, Stable isotope hydrology, deuterium and oxygen-18 in the water cycle: International Atomic Energy Agency, Technical Reports Series No. 210, 339 p.

Ingraham, N.L., and Taylor, B.E., 1991, Light stable isotope systematics of large-scale hydrologic regimes in California and Nevada: Water Resources Research, v. 27, p. 77–90, doi:10.1029/90WR01708, accessed August 21, 2012 at http://www.agu.org/pubs/crossref/1991/90WR01708.shtml.

Izbicki, J.A., Metzger, L.F., McPherson, K.R., Everett, R.R., and Bennett, G.L., 2006, Sources of high-chloride water to wells, eastern San Joaquin ground-water subbasin, California: USGS Open-File Report 2006-1309, 8 p. (Also available at http://pubs.usgs.gov/of/2006/1309/.)

Izbicki, J.A., Stamos, C.L., Metzger, L.F., Halford, K.J., Kulp, T.R., and Bennett, G.L., 2008, Source, distribution, and management of arsenic in water from wells, wastern San Joaquin ground-water subbasin, California: USGS Open-File Report 2008-1272, 8 p. (Also available at *http://pubs.usgs.gov/of/2008/1272/.*)

Jones, S.R., and Garbarino, J.R., 1999, Methods of analysis by the U.S. Geological Survey National Water Quality Laboratory—Determination of arsenic and selenium in water and sediment by graphite furnance-atomic absorption spectrometry: U.S. Geological Survey Open-File Report 98-639, 39 p.

Kalin, R.M., 2000, Radiocarbon dating, *in* Cook, P.G., and Herczeg, A.L., eds., Environmental tracers in subsurface hydrology: Boston, Kluwer Academic Publishers, p. 111–144.

Lucas, L.L., and Unterweger, M.P., 2000, Comprehensive review and critical evaluation of the half-life of tritium: Journal of Research of the National Institutes of Standards and Technology, v. 105, no. 4, p. 541–549.

Michel, 1976, Tritium inventories of the world oceans and their implications: Nature, v. 263, p. 103–106.

Municipal Code Corporation, 2008, Well construction and destruction, title 8, chap. 8.20 *of* Book Publishing Company, eds., Calaveras County, California code of ordinances: County of Calaveras, California, accessed August 21, 2012 at *http://library.municode.com/index.aspx?clientId=16236.*

Schlumberger, Inc, 1972, Log interpretation, Volume 1—principles: New York, Schlumberg Limited, 112 p.

Thatcher, L.L., Janzer, V.J., and Edwards, K.W., 1977, Methods for determination of radioactive substances in water and fluvial sediments: Technology of Water-Resources Investigations of the U.S. Geological Survey, A-5, 95 p.

University of California, 2010, Statewide integrated pest management program, California Weather Database, ©1995–2011 by the Reagents of the University of California (used with permission): University of California, Davis, accessed May 27, 2011 at *http://www.ipm.ucdavis.edu/WEATHER/wxretrieve.html.*

U.S. Environmental Protection Agency, 2009, National primary drinking water regulations: EPA 816-F-09-004, 6 p., accessed August 1, 2011, at *http://water.epa.gov.drink/contaminants.*

U.S. Geological Survey, 2010, National field manual for the collection of water-quality data: U.S. Geological Survey Techniques of Water-Resources Investigations, book 9, chaps. A1–A9. (Also available at *http://pubs.water.usgs.gov/twri9A.*)

Water Resources & Information Management Engineering, Inc. (WRIME), 2003, Calaveras County Water District Camanche/Valley Springs area hydrogeologic assessment: WRIME, Inc., variously paged.

Water Resources & Information Management Engineering, Inc. (WRIME), 2007, Calaveras County Water District Groundwater management plan 2007 update public review draft: WRIME, Inc., variously paged.

Wyllie, M. R. J., Gregory, A. R., and Gardner, L. W., 1956, Elastic wave velocities in heterogeneous and porous media: Geophysics, v. 21, no. 1, p. 41–70.

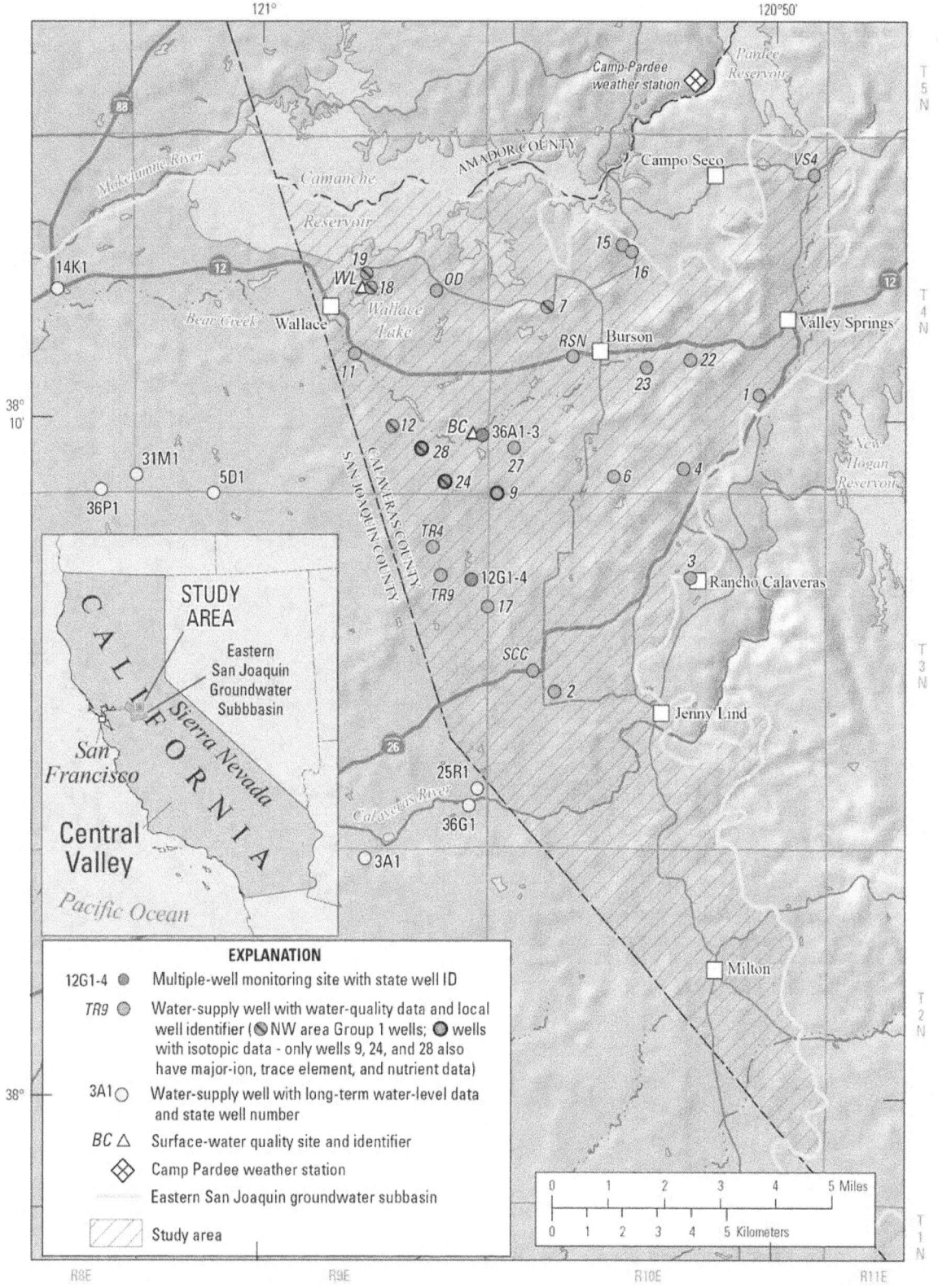

Figure 1. Location of Camanche/Valley Springs area of the Eastern San Joaquin Groundwater Subbasin, Calaveras County, California.

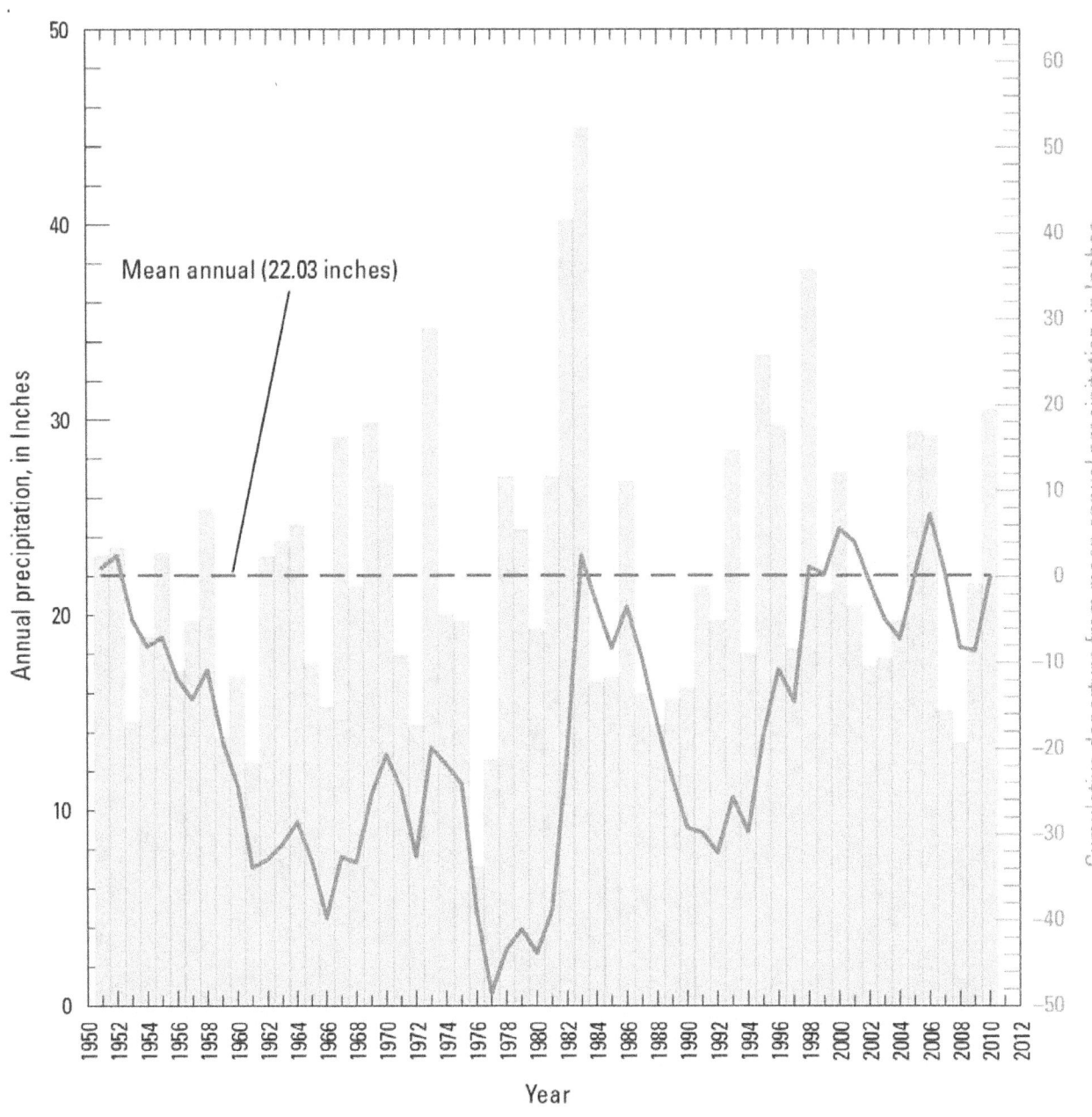

Figure 2. Annual precipitation and cumulative departure from mean annual precipitation at Camp Pardee, Calaveras County, California, 1951–2010.

Figure 3. Exposed lahar deposit near multiple-well site 3N/9E-12G1-4, Camanche/Valley Springs area, Calaveras County, California.

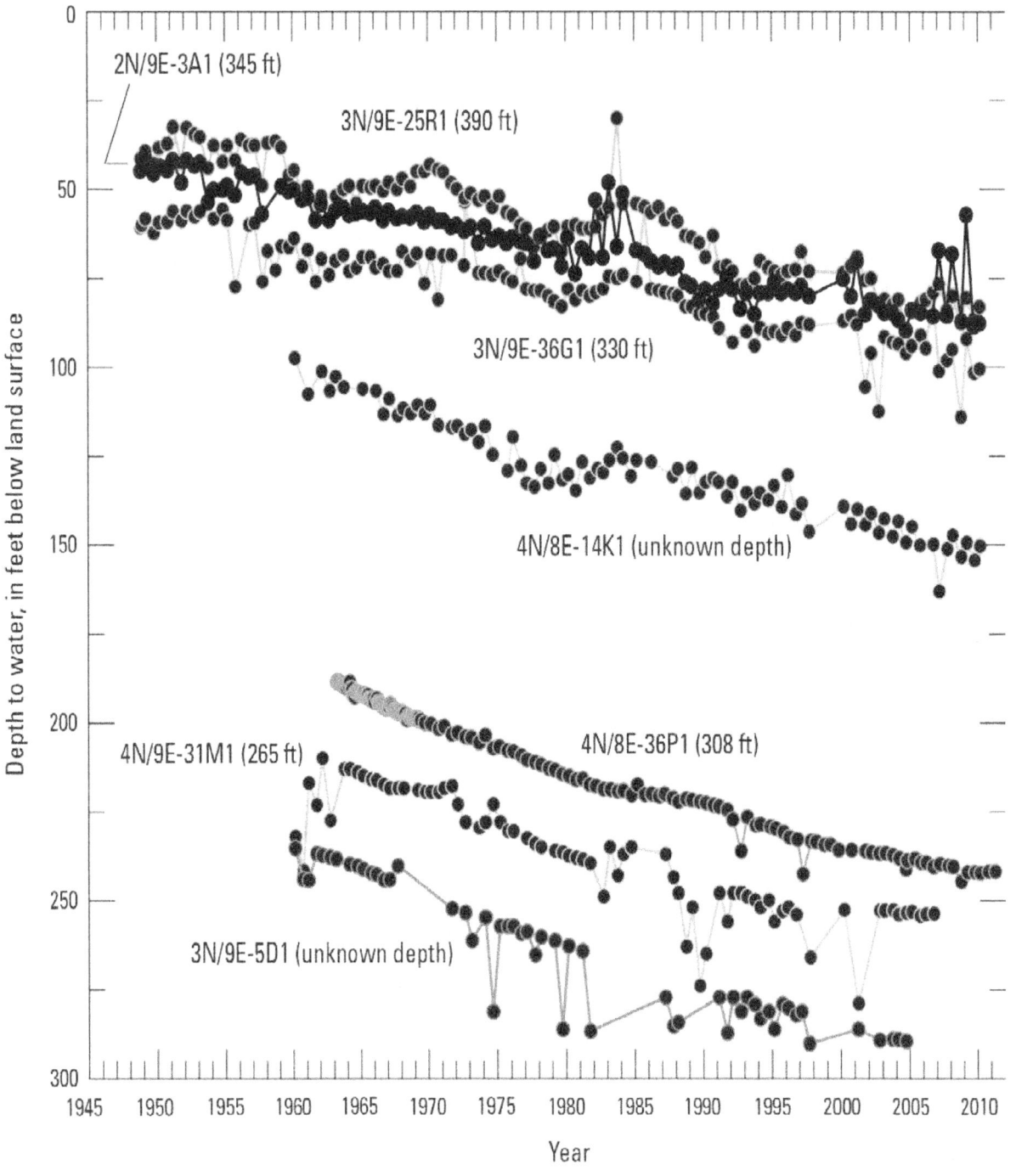

Figure 4. Water levels in selected wells in the Eastern San Joaquin Groundwater Subbasin, California, 1945–2011.

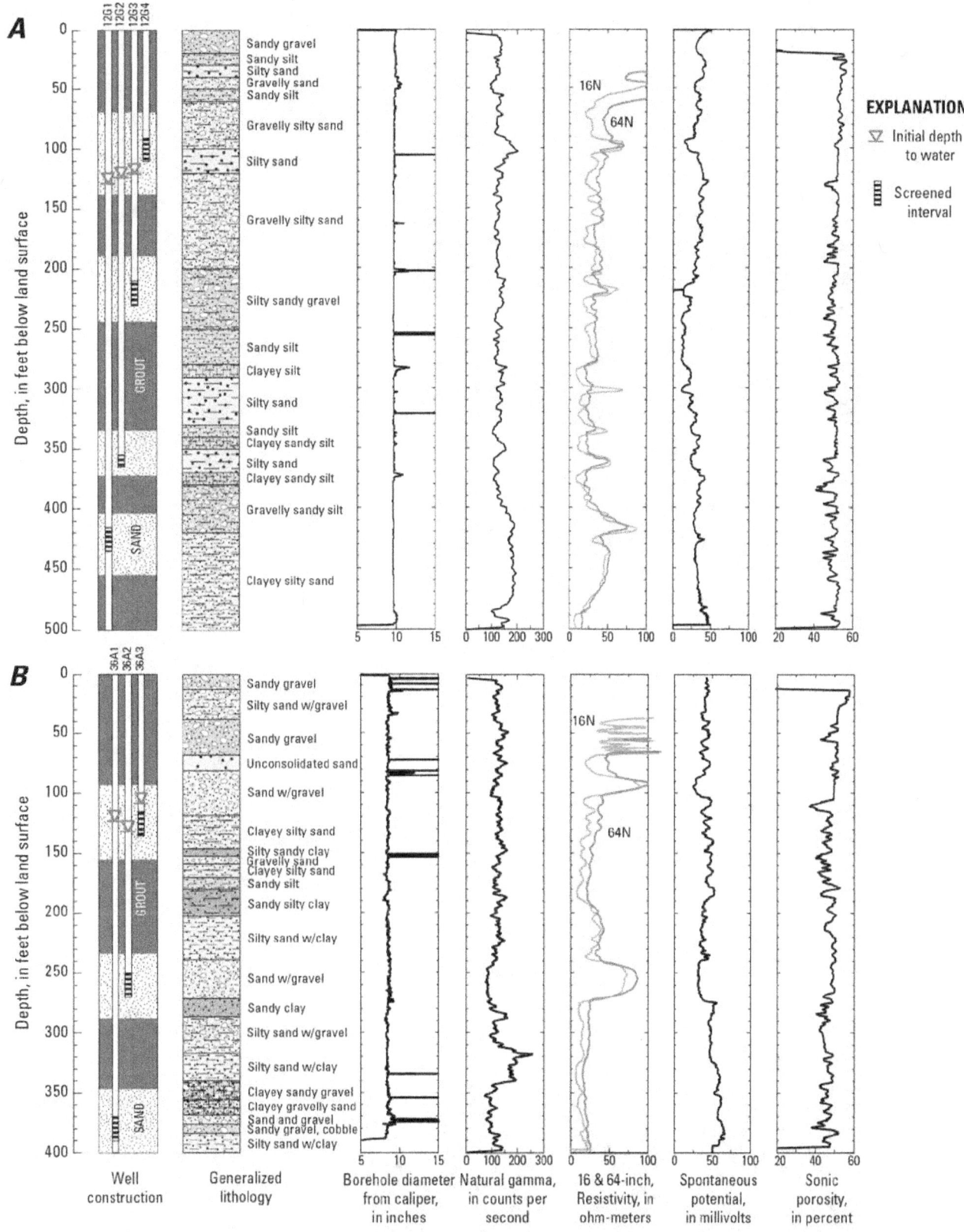

Figure 5. Well construction, lithology, and geophysical logs for multiple-well sites **A**. 3N/9E-12G1-4 and **B**. 4N/9E-36A1-3, Camanche/Valley Springs area, Calaveras County, California.

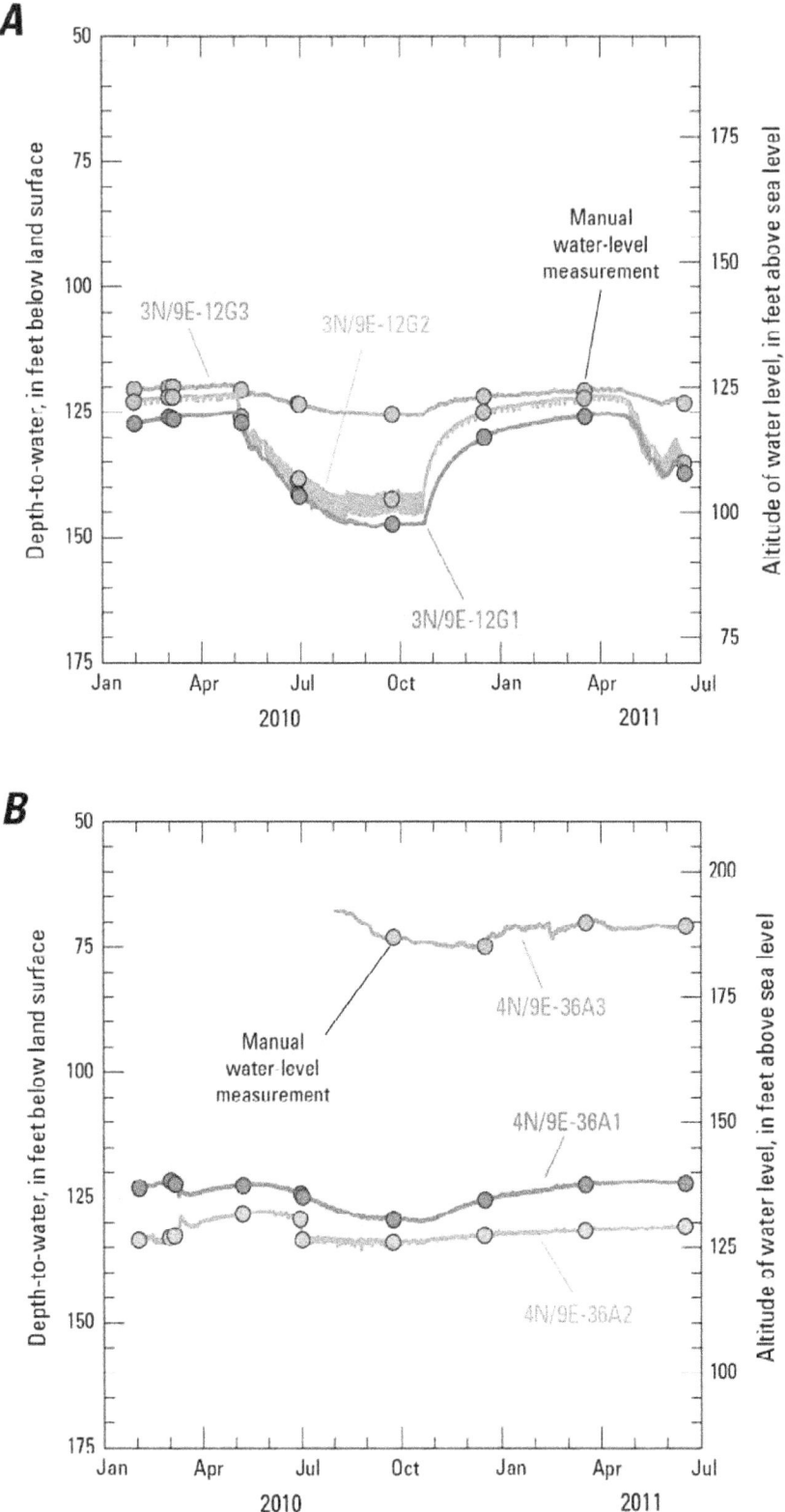

Figure 6. Hydrographs for monitoring wells **A**. 3N/9E-12G1-3, and **B**. 4N/9E-36A1-3, Camanche/Valley Springs area, Calaveras County, California, 2010–11.

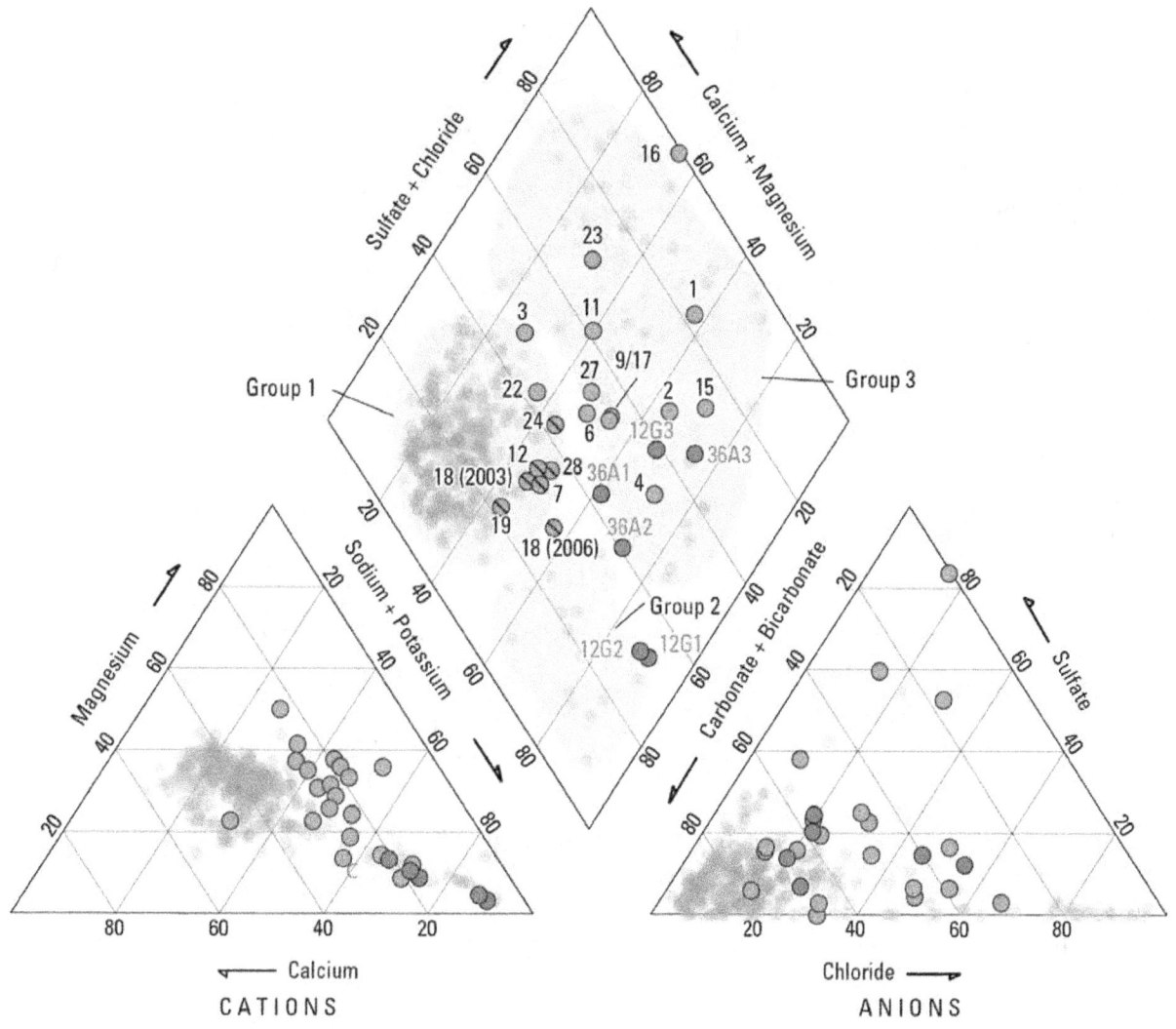

PERCENTAGE OF TOTAL MILLIEQUIVALENTS PER LITER

EXPLANATION

36A1 ● Monitoring well at multiple-well site and identifier

19 ● Water-supply well and identifier (◉ NW area Group 1 well),
sampled in the Camanche/Valley Springs area, 2003–06
(well 18 sampled twice with years shown in parentheses)

● Water-supply well sampled in San Joaquin County, 1969–2005
(Modified from Izbicki and others, 2006)

Figure 7. Major-ion chemistry of water from selected wells in the Eastern San Joaquin Groundwater Subbasin, Calaveras and San Joaquin Counties, California.

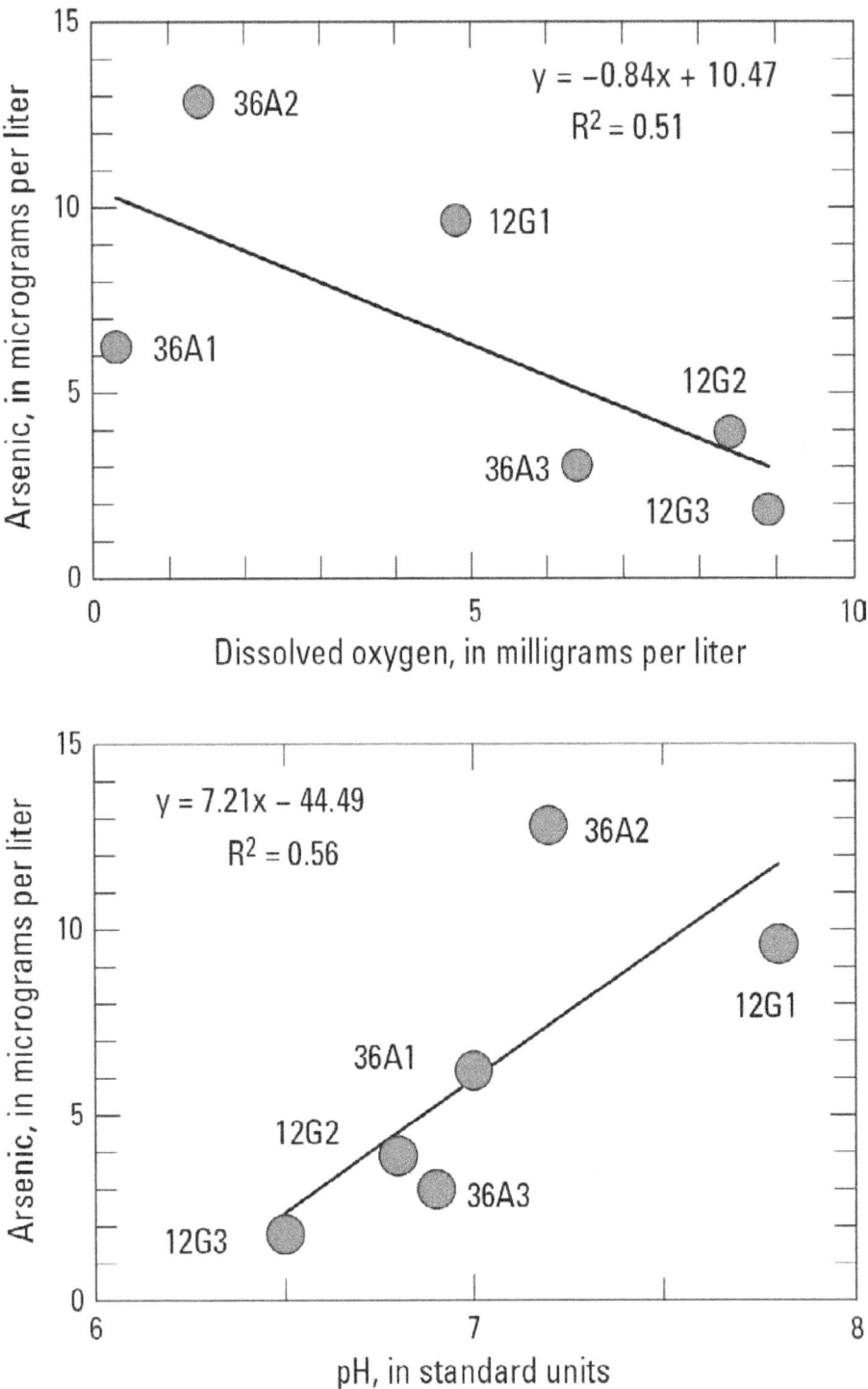

Figure 8. Arsenic as a function of dissolved oxygen (top) and pH (bottom) in water from multiple-well sites, Camanche/Valley Springs area, Calaveras County, California.

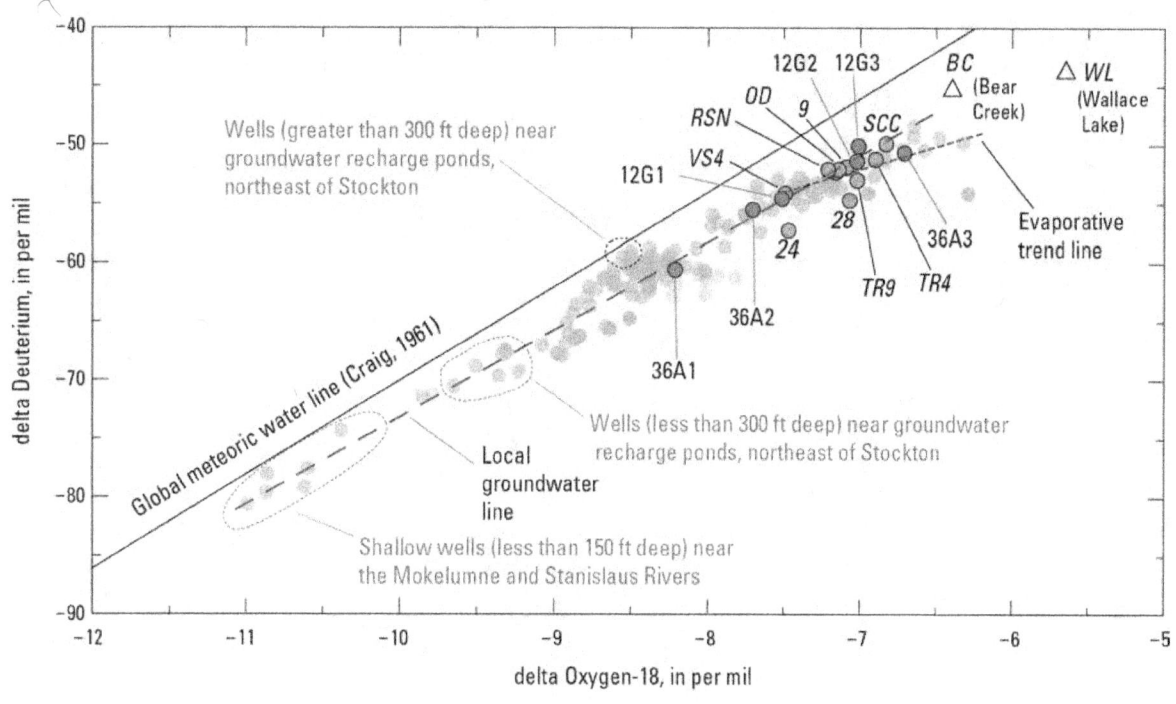

Figure 9. Delta oxygen-18 and delta deuterium composition of water from multiple well and surface water sites in the Camanche/Valley Springs area, and selected wells in the Stockton area, Eastern San Joaquin Groundwater Subbasin, San Joaquin and Calaveras Counties, California.

Table 1. Construction data for monitoring wells at multiple-well sites, Camanche/Valley Springs area, Calaveras County, California.

[See figure 1 for locations (map numbers) of wells. USGS (U.S. Geological Survey) identification number: the unique number for each site in USGS NWIS (National Water Information System) database. Depths in feet below land surface. Land surface altitude in feet above sea level which refers to the National Geodetic Vertical Datum of 1929 (NGVD of 1929).

State well number	USGS site identification number	Depth drilled	Depth cased	Depth of top perforation	Depth of bottom perforation	Land Surface altitude
3N/9E-12G1	380738120555601	503	500	415	435	245
3N/9E-12G2	380738120555602	503	365	355	365	245
3N/9E-12G3	380738120555603	503	230	210	230	245
3N/9E-12G4	380738120555604	503	110	90	110	245
4N/9E-36A1	380946120554401	400	390	370	390	260
4N/9E-36A2	380946120554402	400	270	250	270	260
4N/9E-36A3	380946120554403	400	135	115	135	260

Table 2. Field measurements and laboratory analyses of samples from monitoring wells at multiple-well sites, Camanche/Valley Springs area, Calaveras County, California, June-July 2010.

[See figure 1 for locations of monitoring wells. Parameter code is a five-digit number in the USGS computerized data system, National Water Information System (NWIS), used to uniquely identify a specific constituent or property; not listed where no USGS values are shown. Alkalinity values collected and analyzed by USGS represent field measurements with parameter code 39086; all others represent laboratory analyses where noted. $CaCO_3$, calcium carbonate; uS/cm, microsiemen per centimeter at 25 C; C, degree Celsius; mg/L, milligram per liter; ug/L, microgram per liter; A, average value; E, value estimated; <, actual value is less than value shown; —, no data; ND, not detected]

Parameter or Constituent	Parameter Code	Unit	Monitoring Well						4N/9E-36A1-3 Field Blank
			3N/9E-12G1	3N/9E-12G2	3N/9E-12G3	4N/9E-36A1	4N/9E-36A2	4N/9E-36A3	
Sample Date	—	—	6/28/2010	6/29/2010	6/28/2010	6/30/2010	6/30/2010	7/20/2010	6/30/2010
Dissolved oxygen (field)	(00300)	mg/L	4.8	8.4	8 9	0.3	1.4	6.4	—
pH (field)	(00400)	std units	7.8	6.8	6 5	7.0	7.2	6.9	[1] E 7.1
Specfic conductance (field)	(00095)	µS/cm	221	118	187	246	255	269	[1] < 5
Temperature	(00010)	(°C)	23 5	21.5	22.0	22.5	22.0	26.0	—
Residual On Evapora ion	(70300)	mg/L	220	154	191	212	210	239	< 10
Calcium	(00915)	mg/L	2.96	1.71	6.34	13.7	8.99	7.80	< .044
Magnesium	(00925)	mg/L	.788	.558	2.38	2.99	3.09	2.35	< .016
Potassium	(00935)	mg/L	1.82	2.81	8.15	4.32	4.54	6.69	< .064
Sodium	(00930)	mg/L	42 9	20.0	18.2	30.4	37.6	34.2	< .1
Alkalinity as CaCO3 (field)	(39086)	mg/L	A 65	A 32	A 27	A 66	A 68	A 36	[1] < 8
Bromide	(71870)	mg/L	.06	.05	.11	.06	.07	.20	< .02
Chloride	(00940)	mg/L	13.3	8.59	21.8	15.7	17.2	42.2	< .12
Fluoride	(00950)	mg/L	.34	.20	.09	.21	.24	E .06	< .08
Silica	(00955)	mg/L	97.6	101	97.0	76.5	74.8	87.1	< .1
Sulfate	(00945)	mg/L	12.5	3.00	9.28	26.6	22.2	12.5	< .18
Sulfide	(99119)	mg/L	.1	.1	.3	.1	.1	.3	—
Ammonia plus organic nitrogen	(00623)	mg/L as N	E .07	E .08	< .1	E .08	E .08	.12	< .1
Ammonia	(00608)	mg/L as N	0.24	.06	E .01	.04	.05	< .02	E .01
Nitrate plus nitrite	(00631)	mg/L as N	1.91	2.01	2.09	< .04	.501	1.55	< .040
Nitrite	(00613)	mg/L as N	.002	.002	< .002	< .002	.004	E .002	< .002
Aluminum	(01106)	µg/L	21.0	20.3	18.5	22.0	12.4	39.7	< 3.4
Barium	(01005)	µg/L	14.1	10.7	55.4	28.9	29.7	11.4	< .6
Iron	(01046)	µg/L	10	E 4	8	217	E 4	[2] 1,270	< 6
Lithium	(01130)	µg/L	60.9	48.3	17.2	58.6	29.7	38.7	< .06
Manganese	(01056)	µg/L	2.2	3.8	10.9	[2] 116	11.4	[2] 154	< .2
Strontium	(01080)	µg/L	39 2	26.1	86.8	138	123	64.4	< .4
Arsenic	(01000)	µg/L	9.6	3.9	1 8	6.2	[2] 12.8	3.0	< .044
Boron	(01020)	µg/L	278	100	21	697	303	34	< 2
Iodine	(71865)	mg/L	0.005	< .002	E 0.002	0.024	.012	.002	< .002
Carbon-14 counting error	(49934)	% modern	0.16	0.18	0 27	0.13	0.16	0.29	—
Carbon-14	(49933)	% modern	29.4	40.8	74.7	18.9	30.2	76.0	—
Apparent C-14 age	—	years	9,800	7,200	2,300	13,400	9,600	2,200	—
Tritium	(07000)	pCi/L	[3] ND	[3] ND	[3] ND	[3] ND	[3] ND	[4] 0.52	—
Carbon-13/Carbon-12 ratio	(82081)	per mil	-17.11	-18.80	-17.56	-18.55	-17.60	-19.39	—

[1] Laboratory value

[2] Value equals or exceeds the current maximum contaminant level (MCL) or is outside of the acceptable range for primary or secondary Federal and State drinking-water standards (California Department of Public Health, 2010; U S Environmental Protection Agency, 2009)

[3] Below long term minimum detection level (LT-MDL) of 0 3 pCi/L

[4] Value has one sigma standard deviation of +/- 0 29

Table 3. Summary of delta deuterium and delta oxygen-18 values in samples from selected surface-water sites and groundwater wells, Camanche/Valley Springs area, Calaveras County, California, 2010-11.

[See figure 1 for location of selected surface-water sites and groundwater wells. Parameter code [82085] is a five-digit number in the USGS computerized data system, National Water Information System (NWIS), used to uniquely identify a specific constituent or property. USGS (U.S. Geological Survey) identification number: the unique number for each site in USGS NWIS (National Water Information System) database. Per mil, parts per thousand; —, no data]

Map ID	State well No. (abbreviated or local identifier)	USGS identification No.	Well depth (ft)	Sample date	Delta deuterium (per mil) [82082]	Delta oxygen-18 (per mil) [82085]
		Surface-water sites				
[1]BC	—	380946120554601	—	3/17/2011	-45.1	-6.39
[2]WL	—	381154120575702	—	3/17/2011	-43.6	-5.64
		Wells				
SCC	—	380616120544101	—	6/6/2011	-49.9	-6.83
12G1	3N/9E-12G1	380738120555601	500	6/28/2010	-54.5	-7.50
12G2	3N/9E-12G2	380738120555602	365	6/29/2010	-51.3	-7.01
12G3	3N/9E-12G3	380738120555603	230	6/28/2010	-50.0	-7.00
TR9	—	380740120562901	—	6/6/2011	-53.0	-7.02
TR4	—	380805120563901	—	6/6/2011	-51.2	-6.90
9	—	380853120552401	220	6/6/2011	-51.9	-7.09
24	—	380903120562501	360	6/6/2011	-57.3	-7.47
28	—	380932120565301	320	6/6/2011	-54.7	-7.07
36A1	4N/9E-36A1	380946120554401	390	6/30/2010	-60.5	-8.20
36A2	4N/9E-36A2	380946120554402	270	6/30/2010	-55.5	-7.69
36A3	4N/9E-36A3	380946120554403	135	7/20/2010	-50.6	-6.70
RSN	—	381054120535701	—	6/6/2011	-52.0	-7.21
OD	—	381151120563601	—	6/6/2011	-52.1	-7.14
VS4	—	381335120491401	—	6/6/2011	-54.1	-7.49

[1] Bear Creek
[2] Wallace Lake